Bibliographic information published by the German National Library:

The German National Library lists this publication in the National Bibliography; detailed bibliographic data are available on the Internet at http://dnb.dnb.de .

Imprint:

Copyright © 2014 GRIN Verlag, Open Publishing GmbH
Print and binding: Books on Demand GmbH, Norderstedt Germany
ISBN: 9783668352766

This book at GRIN:

http://www.grin.com/en/e-book/345089/fences-by-august-wilson-a-reflective-essay-on-conflict-family-and

Otivia Headley

**"Fences" by August Wilson. A reflective essay on con-
flict, family, and family therapy**

GRIN Publishing

Final Paper: *Fences*
Otivia Headley
Social Work Practice: Family Treatment SSW 794.00

May 16th 2014

Fences, by August Wilson, is a story enmeshed with conflict surrounding an African American family who lives in Pittsburg Pennsylvania in the year 1957. The center of the conflict seems to be the main character and head of household, Troy Maxson. Troy's conflicts arise with his closest friend Bono, his son Lyons (from a previous relationship), his wife Rose and their son Cory. Each conflict that arises in the story lends a hand to the structure of the Maxson family and the inner/external conflicts that each character plays out.

Troy is the victim of living in a generation where there were limited opportunities for African Americans. Through his experiences he has formed his beliefs that African Americans will always have to struggle to survive and the only thing that they can do is stay practical and support their families the best they can. Troy's conflicts arise because he imposes his views and beliefs onto his family and demands that they view life through his lens. This is in accordance to Dickerson (2013), which states, "Narrative therapists understand, that problems are produced through clients positioning in wider cultural stories or discourses" (pp. 103). In regards to Troy and his relationship with Lyons it is shown from their first encounter how strained their relationship is. Their relationship is strained due to the difference in outlooks that the two characters have adopted. Just as Troy is engulfed with memories from a generation were African Americans were treated poorly, Lyons is growing up in a generation where he views life as more of a place of opportunities for African Americans. Lyons is a struggling musician who feels that his music gives him a sense of belonging and purpose. Troy believes Lyons optimism to be blindness and that difference in beliefs further wedges a gap between the son and father relationship. Troy's distrust in society creates a barrier between his relationship with Lyons and pushes him away. In addition I believe the disconnect between Lyons and Troy stems from the fact that Troy was in prison for the first 15 years of Lyons life. Lyons mentioned in the book that Troy didn't know him and he didn't raise him. Troy's attitude towards his son is out of protection but comes across as ridicule and judgment, which doesn't allow for Lyons to understand or want to further connect with his father.

When Troy was let out of prison he met Rose who became his wife. Throughout the book Rose exemplifies a character with the traits of understand-

2

ing and compassion for Troy as well as for the other characters. Rose puts all her time, effort and faith into her husband and son (Cory), but is stunted when Troy reveals that he has fathered a child (Raynell) by Alberta his secret lover. Rose and Troy's relationship, which seems to start out close, quickly turns distant almost to the point of emotional cut-off.   This is in accordance with Nichols (1988), which states, "Any two people in a relationship go through cycles of closeness and distance" (pp. 145).

While Troy tries to explain that the affair occurred due to him wanting an escape from his life of stress and anxiety, Rose stands up for herself and finally realizes that all her time and effort has been wasted. What furthers the conflict between Rose and Troy is the fact that Raynell's mothers dies and Troy asks for Rose to raise Raynell as her own. Raynell's birth takes Troy and Rose's stable relationship and destabilizes it. The triangulation that stems from Troy's affairs leads to the emotional cut off that occurs between him and his wife. As a result Rose finds her strength in the midst of this conflict as well as forms a bond with Raynell. Being with Troy, Rose felt that she gave up her strength in order for Troy to have his and because of this situation she was able to find herself again.

The conflict in the story that I mostly identify with is the conflict between Troy and Cory. Cory is about 17 or 18 during the beginning of the story and has a passion for football. From the first encounter that is shown between Cory and Troy you get a glimpse of the relationship between the two. Troy's parenting style is harsh and Cory is very passive. From early on in the story Troy is shown trying to teach Cory the importance of responsibility but his style of parenting and way of communication comes across so harsh that the message is lost onto Cory. Conflict arises when Cory wants to play football in hopes of earning a scholarship but is shut down by Troy who believes Cory should work and play football as just a hobby or not at all. Once again Troy's past experiences (not making it in baseball) stunts his belief that Cory could be successful in the sport of football. I am not sure if Troy is hurt from the fact that he was not successful in baseball or if he is jealous of Cory's talent and possible success, but I do believe that, just like with Lyons, Troy is trying to protect Cory from being hurt the way he had been. Although this seems as a good action, the way Troy goes about this is very damaging and further pushes Cory away. Throughout the story even when Troy is belittling Cory, Cory still tries to connect with his father but is met with disconnect which eventually pushes Cory away to the point that he doesn't even want to attend Troy's funeral. Nicholas (1988) states, "the greater the emotional fusion between generations the greater the likelihood of cutoff, some people seek distance by moving far away from their parents others do so emotionally" (pp. 148). A lot of Troy and Cory's relationship mirrors the relationship of Troy and his father. Troy grew up with a father who showed loved through being responsible for his children. He was mean and didn't show any compassion or loving emotion but he didn't leave his children. That is exactly how Troy is but he does not see how just as his fathers actions caused him to run away, the same thing was happening with Cory. This is in accordance to Nicholas (1988), which states, "the problem in the identified patient is a product of the relationship of that persons parent which is a product of their parents continuing back for several generations. The problem is neither the child nor adult but instead the problem is the result of a multigenerational sequence in which all family members are actors and reactors" (pp. 147).

Although the conflicts mentioned above could be seen as major there is a conflict that I believe is significant but not as major. This conflict is between Troy and his best friend Bono. Bono and Troy met while Troy was in jail and was there during Troy's baseball days. Although Bono admired Troy's sense of responsibility and leadership Bono quickly began to change his feelings and became concerned with Troy's marriage. Bono and Troy bump heads on the issue of infidelity and I think Bono's morals and thoughts about loyalty put a wedge between his friendship with Troy. Towards the end of the book Bono stopped coming around and became distant towards Troy. What Bono admired about Troy came to be the reason he became distant. I would consider Bono to be functional kin to Troy which is defined as 'non-biological related family members who have been designated as kin" (Watts-Jones, 1997, pp. 346).

All of the conflicts in the story stem from Troy and his demand that all his loved ones be practical, responsible and loyal, all of which we see him not doing. His affair, his rebellion against his employers and his refusal to see life as it really is instead of the imaginary way he views it in his own head. In regards to any solutions that were attempted by the family I believe both Cory and Lyons

4

tried to mend their relationship with Troy by trying to connect with him on different topics such as sports and work but each time they tried Troy shut down their attempts and further pushed both boys away. I do not think that Troy realized what his actions did to his children emotionally and I also believe that even if he did he would still continue to do so because that is how he was raised. His father didn't show any love and compassion so that is all he knew.

In regards to my family I see a lot of similarity between the relationship of Troy and Cory and the relationship I have with my mother. Like Troy my mother means well but her form of communications doesn't allow for he message to be received well. Being that my mother grew up without a mother at a very young age and was left to be the matriarch of her family at 11 years old it is hard for her to convey her emotions and feelings without being harsh. Tough love is what comes to mind when I think about both sets of relationships and how it takes a toll on the children that are affected. The relationship that I have with my mother is very unpredictable because one day it is fine and we can have a normal conversation and then the next day it is as if we barley know each other. Being a social work student I have been able to use my knowledge to better understand my mother and realize how much her childhood affects her parenting style and herself as an individual who grew up with no guidance. It seems so easy to side with the children such as Cory but it is important to remember that at one point Troy was also a child and went through situations worse than Cory and has adapted the best way he knew how. The only difference that I see between the two relationships is the outcomes. Due to my knowledge I believe that is what keeps me from being emotionally cut off from my mother, it's like as annoyed as I may get I understand that she has a past and may not be able to communicate those feelings or emotions in an appropriate way. Cory wasn't able to understand that and his relationship suffered because of this. Another similarity that my family has with the Maxson family is the significance we both put on responsibility. Troy gives the example that although his father was mean and didn't do much for him and his 11 siblings he was always responsible for them and made sure that they were always cared for unlike his mother who left when he was 8 years old. Both my parents have instilled on to my siblings and I that we should always strive to be responsible individuals. Just like with Troy and his children the message is sometimes lost due to the way it is delivered. When my brother and sister graduated high school my mother automatically wanted them both to go to college, which was not what either of them wanted to do. After months of debate my mother gave them the ultimatum of either going to college, getting a full time job, or leaving her house. Although it seems extremely drastic my mothers end goal was to teach my siblings that nothing in this world is free and it's either you go to school become knowledgeable and get a degree or you get a job and earn a living. The sense of responsibility that came with going to school or working full time would eventually assist in building a stronger charac-ter, prepare you to be an adult and one day allow you to support your own fami-ly. As great as the message was, because of the deliver it just makes the person on the receiving end of the lesson defensive and in turn the message is lost. Both Troy and my mother mean well but their communication skills kill their message and doesn't allow for it to be received well. Both Troy and my mother grew up with less than ideal family situations and have adapted the only way they know how.

As the therapist for the Maxson family I would choose to use a Nar-rative Therapy model. According Lavelle (2014) narrative therapy is concerned with the ways people construct meaning rather than the ways they behave. Lavelle goes on to state that narrative therapy also helps families look for the unhelpful influences of various cultural values and institutions (Slide 2). Being that Narrative therapy helps people interpret their experiences and it's influence on their lives, I believe this model will offer the Maxson family insight on how their interpretations are creating negative wedges in their relationships.

Dickerson (2013) states 'narrative therapists attend to how dis-course shapes peoples understanding of their experiences" (pp. 102). Through this understanding therapists can guide the members of a family through the narrative in a way that would allow for them to separate the problems from the individuals. This is done through the technique of externalizing, which is, can be defined as "locating problems, not within individuals, but as products of culture and history. Problems that is understood to have been socially constructed and created over time" (pp.103). Using the technique of externalizing with the Maxson family will need a lot of work mainly because the family as a whole is so

6

use to making individuals the problem. Troy would say everyone in his life is a problem, starting way back with his father. Hardy (1984) states 'Realties and truths are constructed through social interaction. Post modernism advocates create space for multiple voices to emerge so that each voice may define its experiences – its reality" (pp. 22).

As the family therapist I would create a space for each member to express and use their voice in order to allow for the family to externalize their issues as a family as well as externalize their problems individually. I think it is important for them to all have individual counseling because they each have things that they need to address within themselves before they come together as a group. In regards to the externalizing technique I believe the Maxson family will benefit because it will allow for remove themselves from the problem and see their issues in a different perspective. For example Troy says he feels like a failure because he did not make it in baseball. Even though he blames being an African American as the reason for this failure deep down inside through his monologues it is shown that Troy believes himself to be a failure and that is why he crushes Cory's dream of being a football player so that he could protect his son from the feeling of a being a failure. As the therapist I would acknowledge that he was a baseball player and that when he wasn't able to play professionally that caused a sense of failure. This allows for the feeling of failure to be removed from the client and externalized.

Along with allowing each family member to externalize their problems that they perceive as important I would also use a technique of rephrasing. As the therapist I would allow for the Maxson family to verbalize their problems and then re-phrase the narrative in a disconnected way. For example Troy feels like he has been standing in the same position for years and hasn't grown therefore he feels because he is stagnate he is a failure. I would offer the suggestion that rather than being a failure, Troy has succeeded in taking care of his family and being a responsible adult, which he had always wanted to be. This would allow him to see that although he may have been viewing his life one way there are different lens that he can see his life from. This technique could work on the different individuals in the family as well as the family as a whole.

Lastly I would like for the whole family to attend a few sessions and allow for each person to say their narrative and speak their own truth. As each family member speaks I would navigate the conversation giving minimal insight but still being a sense of support there that will redirect the conversation when necessary. By posing questions that challenge prior beliefs and concepts I will help reveal maladaptive behaviors that the individuals in the family may not be conscious of. Also by allowing each person to tell their story it will allow for them to be heard and for conversation to become created because it may spark an interest in someone else. For example if Troy is telling his narrative Cory might be able to see why his behavior is the way it is and it will be less destructive because the person speaking is not being direct, which can eliminate any defensive responses. This is accordance with Nichols (2006), which states "Instead of focusing on patterns of family interaction, constructivism shifted the emphasis to exploring and reevaluating the perspectives that people with problems have about them. Meaning itself became the primary target" (pp. 285).

Russell (2004) sates ' the person is not the problem; the problem is the problem' (pp.3). Using these techniques I would hope that by separating the problem from the person it would allow the individuals to converse in a more healthy matter and instead of being made at the people in the family they can focus their energy on the problems itself. Understanding that a problem cannot define a person but rather it is just something that a person has, may transform the relationships in the Maxson family and mend the ones that have been hostile, cut off or distant.

References

Dickerson, V. (2013). Patriarchy, power and privilege: A narrative/post structural view of work with couples. *Family Process.* Vol 52, 102-114

Hardy, K., & Laszoffy, T.A. (1984). Deconstructing Race in Family Therapy. *Journal of Feminist Family Therapy.* Haworth Press.

Lavelle, L. *Narrative Therapy* [PowerPoint Slides]. Retrieved from Lecture Notes Online Web site: https://bbhosted.cuny.edu/bbcswebdav/pid-16507041-dt-content-rid-60584549_1/courses/HTR01_SSW_79400_01_1142_1/Narrative%20Therapy%20copy.pdf

Nichols, M. & Schwartz, R.C. (1988). Chapter 5, *Family Therapy: Concepts and Methods,* 3rd Edition. New York: Allyn and Bacon.

Nichols, M.P., (2006). Family therapy in the 21st century. In Nichols & Schwam (Eds.), *Family therapy concepts and methods (*Seventh edition), Chapter II, pp. 281-318.

Russell, S. & Carey, M. (2004). Chapter 1: Externalizing; Chapter 2; Re-Authoring. Narrative Therapy; Responding to your questions

Watts-Jones, D. (1997). Toward an African American Genogram. *Family Process.* Vol 36, 375-383

Watts-Jones, D. (2010) Opening the door to dialogue on intersectionality in the therapy process. In *Family Process, Vol 49*

YOUR KNOWLEDGE HAS VALUE